IMAGES

of America

CHICAGO LAWN/
MARQUETTE MANOR

This easily recognizable view of 63rd and Kedzie dates back to February of 1924. Less than 15 years earlier, when a door-to-door fruit and vegetable man named Jim built a small sweet shop on this corner, he was chided for not using better judgment. Kedzie then was considered the outskirts of town.

IMAGES
of America

CHICAGO LAWN/
MARQUETTE MANOR

Kathleen J. Headley

ARCADIA
PUBLISHING

Published by Arcadia Publishing
Charleston, South Carolina

Library of Congress Catalog Card Number: 2001093317

For all general information contact Arcadia Publishing at:
Telephone 843-853-2070
Fax 843-853-0044
E-mail sales@arcadiapublishing.com
For customer service and orders:
Toll-Free 1-888-313-2665

Visit us on the Internet at www.arcadiapublishing.com

This early 1900s postcard suggests the rapid growth of the fledgling community. By the time this postcard was made, Chicago Lawn had grown into a well-established section of Chicago, yet it continued to act as an individual community and did not take on the aspects of a large city.

CONTENTS

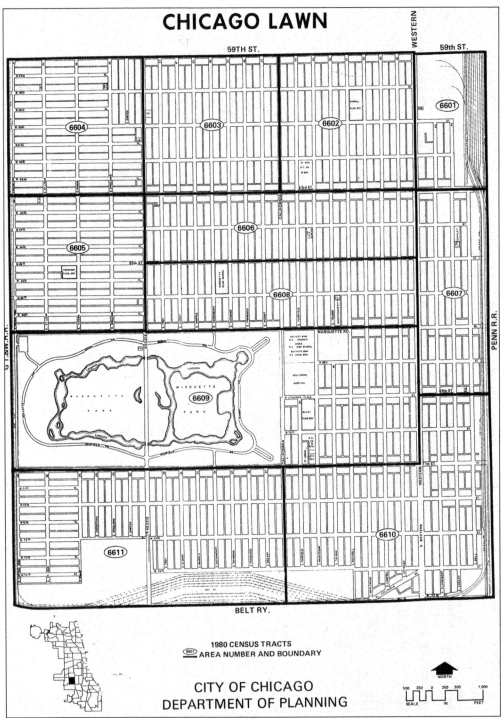

CHICAGO LAWN

WESTERN

59TH ST.

59th ST.

6601

6604

6603

6602

CALIFORNIA

6605

6606

6608

6607

PENN R.R.

MARQUETTE RD.

MARQUETTE PARK

6609

MARQUETTE PARK

CALIFORNIA

WESTERN

BELT RY.

6611

6610

S. WESTERN

BELT RY.

1980 CENSUS TRACTS
6601 AREA NUMBER AND BOUNDARY

CITY OF CHICAGO
DEPARTMENT OF PLANNING

NORTH

500 250 0 250 500   1,000
SCALE   IN   FEET

The City of Chicago does not recognize Marquette Manor as a community on its own. In this census map it is included as the eastern half of Chicago Lawn. Yet all who have lived there know that the strength, enterprise, and uniqueness of Marquette Manor have earned it the right to be listed as one of the two neighborhoods of the Marquette Park area.

INTRODUCTION

"This is where I want to be," wrote then superintendent of county schools John Eberhart, penning a letter to his wife as he traveled through the prairies southwest of Chicago in the mid-1800s. The future he envisioned for himself would become a reality, and the man who would later be deemed the "Father of Chicago Lawn" would leave a lasting legacy on those prairies.

The area surrounding Marquette Park is made up of two neighborhoods—Chicago Lawn and Marquette Manor.

While the boundaries of the two are negotiable, depending on where one lives and in which decade, the City of Chicago defines the boundaries as Bell Avenue on the east, Central Park on the west, and 59th Street south to the Belt Railway, or approximately 75th Street.

Chicago Lawn, sitting on the western end, was founded by educator-turned-real estate developer Professor John Frederick Eberhart. Eberhart came to Illinois from Pennsylvania in 1855, at the age of 25. Within four years, he was elected the first Cook County Superintendent of Schools. There were 198 teachers in Cook County at the time, and Eberhart visited each one of them once a year, traveling by horse and buggy along the rough roads.

As he became familiar with the territory, he was convinced of the great opportunity for development around Chicago. The southwest area was his favorite. The professor made up his mind that when his term was up as superintendent, he'd try his hand in the real estate business.

In 1871, Eberhart bought the property that now extends from 63rd to 67th Streets and from Kedzie to Central Park Avenues. He persuaded one of his good friends, former Chicago Chief of Police James Webb, to buy another large tract running between 63rd and 59th, from Kedzie to Central Park. These two pieces of property formed what would be the original town of Chicago Lawn in the Township of Lake.

Eberhart realized that if his project was to be a success, he must provide transportation to the settlers, most of whom would be working people from Chicago. His first move was to sell the officials of the Chicago, Danville, and Vincennes Railway on the idea of building a trunk line running through his envisioned suburb to the city.

Eberhart paid the railroad $5,000 for the line, but the contract provided that the railroad give three-year passes to those persons who either aided in the construction of the road or who became residents along the line. It took three years to complete. And when the road was ready, Eberhart christened his new suburb Chicago Lawn, although the early settlers would refer to it simply as "The Lawn."

Marquette Manor, on the eastern end, got a much later start due in part to wealthy and eccentric landowner Hetty Green, who had acquired a good portion of the land east of Kedzie and north of 67th Street through foreclosures in 1877. While a few farms dotted the land, and one building, Pryor's General Store, sat on what is now 63rd Place and Western, most of the land lay undeveloped and uninhabited.

In 1905, Archbishop James Quigley extended an invitation to the Augustinian Friars to service the Catholic population in the prairies southwest of downtown. A 5-acre tract of land on 63rd Street, just east of Hetty Green's holdings, sitting between Oakley and Claremont Avenues, was purchased. Rev. James Green arrived here from New York on June 24, 1905, and

7

set about the task of building a monastery, chapel, and college for boys.

Perhaps the largest problem facing Father Green was one which stifled the growth of this vast expanse of land, which would become known as Marquette Manor. The problem was Hetty Green and her refusal to improve the land with a proper sewage system or sell the land to another who could improve it. Father Green's concern for the health of his fledgling congregation and the future of the area drove him into bitter controversy and an eventual court battle, which ended in triumph over the wealthy landowner.

The story of Marquette Manor could not be complete without giving credit for the extensive growth of the southern portion to the Sisters of St. Casimir and their foundress, Mother Maria Kaupas. Also here at the invitation of Archbishop Quigley, the SSCs, with the help of Rev. Anthony Staniukynas, acquired the property on 67th Street between Rockwell and Washtenaw Avenues and commenced building the SSC Motherhouse, which would also house the St. Casimir Academy. Upon the arrival of the Lithuanian order of the SSCs and the institutions they would foster, Marquette Manor also became an entry point for Lithuanian immigrants and remains so today.

The neighborhoods of Chicago Lawn and Marquette Manor surround Marquette Park, which has served as a centerpiece and common denominator for both communities. From its grand beginning, the 323-acre park with its 3 1/2 miles of lagoon, golf course, ball fields, tennis courts, flower gardens, and playgrounds has earned its reputation as the playground of the Southwest Side.

Both neighborhoods experienced substantial growth during the 1920s as retail establishments, institutions, and houses sprouted up. By the middle of the 20th century, the area was considered fully populated.

The 1950s were an almost idyllic time as Chicago Lawn and Marquette Manor settled into the business of working and raising families.

The area surrounding Marquette Park experienced a rather turbulent entry into the latter quarter of the 20th century and unfortunately acquired national notoriety and a reputation for the racial strife imposed by outside groups. Open housing marches drew the ire of local residents and resulted in rock throwing and protests. Community groups worked overtime. But the marches and rallies continued to cast a dark shadow on the once-tranquil community.

And then, as the 1970s turned into the 1980s, committed residents were winning the fight against redlining and other unscrupulous practices. As the 1990s came to a close, Chicago Lawn and Marquette Manor were bearing the fruits of the tireless efforts of community organizations.

Even though the Marquette Park area has achieved an ethnic and racially diverse state, a strong Lithuanian influence is still prevalent and keeps renewing itself as another wave of young immigrants from the Baltic state make this area their home.

One

CHICAGO LAWN
IN THE BEGINNING

The early settlers were at the mercy of the weather. Winters in the late 1800s were severe. Snow fell early in October and stayed on the ground almost all winter. After the spring thaw, paths were rough, muddy, and generally impassable. Once dried up by the sun, the ruts from wagons still remained, making it difficult to walk anywhere, especially when carrying a parcel.

Rainfalls filled the ditches on the side of the roads and often brought flooding. It was not unusual for the wooden plank sidewalks to dislodge and float away. In the absence of rain, the summer sun baked the dirt roads, and the slightest breeze brought clouds of dust.

In 1888, the town of Chicago Lawn boasted two retail establishments on its business block. Before another 20 years was up, businesses would line both sides of the street, and city services would soon make it a bit easier to handle the severe prairie weather.

John F. Eberhart, the man who would become known as the "Father of Chicago Lawn," saw beauty and potential in the prairie land southwest of Chicago. At a time when others were still buying an acre of land from the government for $1.25, Eberhart paid $500 an acre for a wilderness of prairie, mud, and cabbages. Although his initial outlay may sound a bit too speculative, over the years it paid off quite handsomely.

The railroad provided the impetus needed to jump-start the new community. In 1876, Eberhart erected the first building in Chicago Lawn—this depot at 63rd and Central Park. On the first floor was a waiting room, ticket office, and kitchen. The second floor contained living rooms and became the home of Eberhart's parents, Abraham and Elsie, and his sister Sadie, who donated their services as station agents.

Next to the railroad depot Eberhart put his real estate office. So confident was Eberhart of the future of Chicago Lawn that he built all of the original houses himself. He then added additional incentives to perspective home builders by offering the three-year pass on the train to the city and a free 25-foot lot to all buyers of one or more lots.

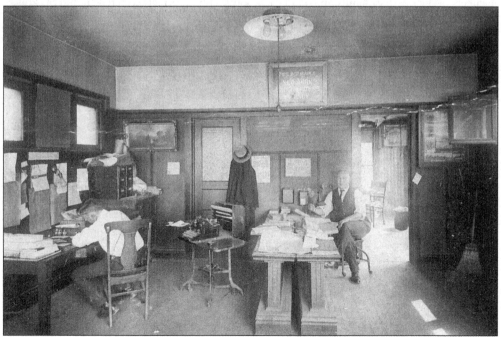

Pictured here is the interior of the Eberhart Real Estate office. Eberhart boldly predicted that Chicago Lawn would have "30 houses, and the lots would be worth $200 each," but most people considered this just the dream of a real estate speculator. Working at his desk on the left is Clarence Hershberger, and seated on the right is John J. Eberhart.

11

Eberhart built his own home, this brick structure at 3415 West 64th Street, which still stands today. Five years later, the tiny settlement was made up of nine houses, many of them home to members of the Eberhart family and all of them south of 63rd Street clustered around St. Louis.

Mrs. John Eberhart is tending her chickens in the back yard of their home in 1901. Surrounding the fledgling community was prairie. One pioneer recalled, "On a clear day, we could see the Village of Englewood."

Evelyn and Willie Eberhart are at the pump about 100 feet from the Frank Eberhart home in 1900. Frank built his home across the street from John.

John Eberhart's daughter Corrine (Maneikis) plays with her dominos in her room.

This 1892 photo shows Amos Cravener's Grocery Store at the corner of 63rd Street and Central Park. This was the first building erected north of 63rd Street. The grocery store was in the front and the meat market in the rear. On the left side of the photo, Cravener's horse and delivery cart await their next call.

This is the meat market in the back of Cravener's store. The photo was taken about 1895. Young Don Cravener is in the white shirt. Next to him is Becker Lewis.

This picture taken inside the Cravener Store about 1900, shows Mrs. Amos Cravener, Albert Dutton, and young Don Cravener. A glance at a 1900 grocery store advertisement gives an idea of the prices. A 5-pound jar of jelly was 13¢. Twenty pounds of corn meal was 25¢. New Orleans molasses were 30¢ a quart, and American Family soap was a nickel a bar.

The funeral concierge of E.O. Weldon awaits the funeral train at the Chicago Lawn Station. They traveled via the Grand Trunk and Western Railroad for internment at Mount Greenwood Cemetery. Mel Bodgett, the town's undertaker, did carpentry and building work when not officiating at funerals.

In 1888, a volunteer fire department was organized. Fred Harold, known as "the big butter and egg man of the day," was the fire chief.

The engine house was located at what is now 62nd Place and St. Louis. The "engine" was a pushcart affair that needed to be pumped by hand. The only water available for fighting fires was well water or that which had accumulated in ditches. Luckily, the early blazes were only prairie fires.

Fred is pictured here with his early volunteers inside the engine house.

In 1892, the Chicago Lawn Rapid Transit Company was formed, and a horsecar line was built to run between Central Park and Ashland Avenue. The trolley was a welcome addition for the residents, even though it afforded no heat in the winter.

In 1889, the early residents of Chicago Lawn voted to annex to the City of Chicago. Although still separated from the big city by miles of prairie, the annexation would eventually bring city services that were sorely needed. The first city water came to Chicago Lawn in 1898, and everybody came out for the event. This is the corner of 63rd and St. Louis with the Wessel Building on the right.

A parade began the Fourth of July celebration in Chicago Lawn in 1898. Parades and music were quite popular in the early days of the Lawn. Nearly every important event was cause for a parade—from the first streetcar to the arrival of city water.

P.D. Hagerman owned the Lawn Club Hall. The first floor housed P.D.'s dry goods store. In 1909, the first library station opened in Chicago Lawn, and P.D. became the librarian. Located on about a half-dozen bookshelves in the rear of Hagerman's Dry Goods Store in the 3500 block of West 63rd Street was a collection of about 1,200 books loaned by the main library downtown.

The Chicago Lawn Band was organized in 1906, under the direction of Chicago Lawn resident and Civil War veteran Professor James A. Beach. Early residents would gather around the Lawn Club Hall to hear the amateur musicians play concerts from the cupola of the building. The band played for church socials, home entertainment, and lectures—upon invitation and without charge.

Before city water reached the little suburb, its residents got along with wells and cisterns. In the 1880s, early settler D.F. Larkin sunk a deep artesian well at the south end of town near the railroad tracks. The water furnished by this well was said to be valuable for its medicinal qualities. Many lots were sold in the Lawn on the strength of that one fact.

Supplies and staples came to Chicago Lawn via the railroad. This photo was taken as local merchant A.E. Schlieske was on his way back from picking up a railroad shipment for his hardware store. The building behind Schlieske was used as a storehouse for goods coming off the railroad cars.

In 1902, residential telephone service came to Chicago Lawn. The switchboard was installed in the home of the first operator, May Blair, pictured here third from the left. There were 19 subscribers who paid $1.50 per month for local service. A call to Chicago was long distance. Standing in front of Delfeld's store with May are: Edith Delfeld, Loretta McCormick, Kate Delfeld, Robert Robson, Clarence Lundy, and Clara Miller.

By 1910, D.F. Larkin was supplying the people of Chicago Lawn with building and heating materials from his Coal and Lumber Yard. Looking east on 63rd Street from the Grand Trunk tracks, his business is visible on the right.

Grocer Julius Wessel came to Chicago Lawn at the prodding of George Hilsman, a schoolboy friend who bought a little cottage home at 61st and St. Louis. Wessel erected the structure pictured here, a huge building for its time, stretching north on St. Louis and then east on 63rd Street. It was so big that the people of the Lawn referred to it as the Wessel Block.

This is Christmas with Julius Wessel and his family in the early 1900s. Julius is standing on the left, and Grandmother Wessel is sitting in front of him.

The Wessel Building had three storefronts, and one of them was home to Lipp's Bakery. Emil Lipp advertised "fresh, clean and wholesome goods, straight from the oven."

Baker Lipp and his family pose outside their establishment.

H.E. Cain opened his drug store on the southeast corner of 63rd and St. Louis, right across from the Wessel Building. As of this printing, it is the oldest retail building in Chicago Lawn.

By the time this picture was taken, the 63rd Street business block was beginning to offer a more diverse array of shopping. Standing inside of Cain's Pharmacy is R.I. Heermans (on the left) and H.E. Cain (on the right).

Cosmo "Charlie" D'Andrea came to America in 1902, at the age of 17. Although young, he had been a shoemaker for four years in his native Palermo, having learned the trade from his father and grandfather. Charlie settled in Chicago Lawn and opened his Shoe Repair Shop at 63rd and Homan in 1908.

For decades, the scissors grinder and knife sharpener made his rounds in Chicago neighborhoods. In this early photo, he is working in back of a Chicago Lawn home.

This 1910 photograph taken by Frank Eberhart shows 65th Place just west of St. Louis. In 1903, an act passed by the state legislature required automobiles to come to a full stop upon nearing any horse-drawn vehicle. The law was enacted as a safeguard against accidents known to have occurred when horses became frightened by the approach of motor cars. The speed of automobiles was limited to 15 miles per hour.

Early residents Mr. and Mrs. W.A. Pickering are pictured in their Chicago Lawn home, located at 6354 South Troy, in about 1910.

Rose Kuhn and her baby doll visit with Ruth Clinton (Kramer) in 1910, on the steps of the E.B. Clinton home at 3328 West 61st Place.

This 1910 photo was taken from Homan Avenue looking east down 64th Street. Notice the wooden planks over the ditches leading from the dirt sidewalks to the dirt roads.

In this 1911 photo, Dick Helwig, Louis Heermans, and Eric Johnson are sitting on a pile of bricks taken from the street when the sewer was put in. The building in the left rear of the picture is the Chicago Lawn Post Office Station at 63rd and St. Louis.

The Lawn Theater, located at 3419 West 63rd Street, was the first of its kind in Chicago Lawn. Before the theater was two years old, John Eberhart died at the age of 84. Almost 50 years had lapsed since he began his tiny settlement with nine houses. Eberhart lived to see his prediction of 20 houses in Chicago Lawn come true and then double, triple, and quadruple.

Two

MARQUETTE MANOR IN THE BEGINNING

In the late 1800s, Western Avenue was only a long, cleared path made of dirt and sand. But even then it was the longest road in the nation. The corner of 63rd and Western was considered the halfway point from Blue Island to city hall. Pryor's General Store sat at what would be 6437 South Western and was sometimes referred to as the halfway house. Funerals processing by carriage stopped at Pryor's, as did farmers on their way to the Blue Island Market. Some spent the night, others just stopped to weigh their hay on the big scale out front. Voters from Archer Avenue south and from State Street west voted at the polling place at Pryor's. Even Mayor Edward Kelly frequented the store as a little boy.

From the Village of Englewood on the east to St. Louis Avenue on the west, large expanses of undeveloped land full of wild strawberries and mushrooms divided farmland. Pryor's sat alone as an outpost in the ruff. (Artist interpretation by Robert Kubkowski.)

Rev. James Green OSA arrived by streetcar in June of 1905, and set about the arduous task of establishing the first Catholic parish to serve the area. The driver of the streetcar, John Bracken, hurried home that night to tell his family about this new parish that would be called St. Rita.

Here Fathers A. Skripka, P. Serafinas, and A. Staniukynas are standing on the site of the future Sisters of St. Casimir Motherhouse. With the help of these Lithuanian priests, land was purchased between 1907 and 1909 for a small group of nuns from Pennsylvania. Led by Mother Maria Kaupas, the SSC's influence would have a great impact on the development and growth of Marquette Manor.

The Augustinians purchased a 5-acre tract of land on 63rd Street between Oakley and Claremont Avenues to become the site of a monastery, a chapel, and a college for boys. Father Green laid the cornerstone on October 26, 1905, and by the fall of 1906, the school was ready to open its doors. The chapel within served as the first church for the parishioners of St. Rita of Cascia.

Progress on the building of the SSC Motherhouse was slowed by the incessant rainy weather. With no drainage system yet in place, the marshy grounds turned to swamps and sometimes prevented the workmen from even getting to their work site.

Completed in 1911, the Motherhouse was now ready for the new Chicago-founded Order of the Sisters of St. Casimir. Also housed in the building was a chapel and the new St. Casimir Academy for high school girls.

No doubt these men were the envy of their Marquette Manor neighbors. Although bicycle clubs were quite popular, bicycling was an expensive sport in the early 1900s.

In the early years, families grew all of their own vegetables to supplement the dry goods purchased from local merchants. In 1912, the Landmichls posed in the garden of their home at 2644 West 59th Street. However, the Landmichls garden was bigger than most, for they also ran a nursery.

Late in the summer of 1915, the Mission Board of the English District canvassed the Marquette Manor and Chicago Lawn area to see if there were enough Lutheran Christians to warrant a new mission in this western part of Chicago. On the first Sunday in October 1916, the first service of what would become known as Hope Evangelical Lutheran Church was held in this storefront at 2552 West 63rd Street.

As the small congregation of St. Rita Church grew, another 5-acre tract of land was purchased between Fairfield and Washtenaw Avenues, 63rd to 62nd Streets. Here a new church-school combination, built in 1915, would capture first place in the Architectural Exhibit of the Art Museum of Chicago in the summer of 1916. Fr. Meaney OSA, assistant to Fr. Green, posed in front of the new building with his car.

At the wheel of his Model T truck is John Hellmuth. Kegs and barrels for flour, pickles, and sugar sitting in the stores lining 63rd Street in the early days were made at his factory. The Hellmuth Cooperage Company was at 53rd and Western right next to the Clausen Pickle Company. Hellmuth, who became wealthy as most businessmen did during those early years, was also a founding member of St. Clare of Montefalco parish.

Taken at the corner of 63rd and Western in 1918, the Marquette Manor "Boys" posed for a picture in front of Roma Drug Store. From left to right are: Frank Barazantni, Shorty Zaleski, Frank Solomon, Unidentified, John Moran, ? Carsher, Arthur Moynihan, Henry McCauley, Unidentified, Louis Briody, and Charles McCarthy.

The Marquette Manor "Boys" posed again on the other side of 63rd and Western. Notice the advertisements for Schlitz Beer on the façade of Schmidt's Buffet.

Two early teachers at St. Rita College were Frs. Harris and Hammond. This picture, taken in 1919, shows a two-flat in the background. Once Hetty Green was defeated in court, a building boom started in Marquette Manor with dozens of these two-flats and bungalows springing up.

SSC Foundress Mother Maria Kaupas posed for a photo with her General Council in 1922. Pictured here are: (seated) Sr. M. Josepha, Mother Maria, Sr. M. Dolorossa; (standing) Sr. M. Vincenta, Sr. M. Concepta, Sr. M. Gertrude, and Sr. M. Rita.

Before Nativity BVM Grammar School opened, the Sisters of St. Casimir conducted an elementary school for boys and girls of Lithuanian heritage in what would later become the St. Casimir Academy Fine Arts Building. Upon the death of Rev. A. Staniukynas, the children collected enough funds to build this statue in his honor.

Rev. A. Briska conducted the eulogy of Father Staniukynas on the grounds of the Motherhouse while the elementary school children look on.

Built in 1921, the Western Avenue Water Tunnel received a hearty welcome. Named after Mayor William Hale Thompson, the new pumping station was one of the improvements Rev. James Green fought for and subsequently received after Hetty Green was forced to give up her holdings in the area.

The immense tunnel at 61st Street allowed this worker to drive right through.

This 1921 view looking southwest from the trestle of the 61st Street shaft of the Western Avenue Tunnel captures a good portion of Marquette Manor at the time. The building boom that escalated in 1920 turned this former hunting ground into a subdivision. Looking very closely, where Marquette Manor meets the horizon, the SSC Motherhouse can be seen on the far left and St. Rita Grammar School on the far right.

Along with the building boom came many amenities. This combination bowling alley and billiard hall advertised, "the elimination of unpleasant cathartics," saying, "The bending and stooping necessary to play either game exercises the muscles directly over the digestive organs, stimulating them to function in a normal healthy manner. Most bodily ills are attributed to any sluggishness in these organs." Western Avenue Recreation enjoyed many subsequent decades of popularity.

In this Sunday morning photo, looking west on 63rd Street from Oakley, parishioners are arriving for Mass at the St. Rita Chapel.

The Moynihan brothers, pictured here, along with Brendan O'Connell were original altar boys serving Sunday Mass with Father Green at St. Rita.

In 1925, the Marquette Park State Bank moved into these quarters at 6314–20 South Western Avenue. The new facility was billed as the "Palace of Banks." Their slogan was "Where familiar faces bank." The institution flourished in the late '20s, with assets topping $3,000,000. But as with many financial institutions, Marquette Park State Bank did not survive the Great Depression.

Taken the year of the opening of the new building, the officers of Marquette Park State Bank are (left to right): Michael Maisel, Vice-President; Brendan O'Connell, Cashier; William Brietzke, President; John W. Utesch, Assistant Cashier; and Miss Cecilia Durkin, Assistant Cashier.

The St. Rita Grammar School Orchestra was always ready for a parade. Formed in 1918, its numbers grew dramatically over the years. Sr. Rose Eleanor OP was the music teacher for this orchestra in the late '20s.

The SSC Motherhouse was actually built in four parts, with the final addition in 1970. This 1926 photo shows the second addition from the rear. On the right side of the photo is a cottage built for nuns suffering from tuberculosis.

By 1920, about 200 Lithuanian families had settled in Marquette Manor, and by 1927, that figure had more than doubled. A committee representing this group began tirelessly petitioning the Archdiocese for the establishment of a Lithuanian National parish within Marquette Manor. A delay came about when some committee members insisted the parish site should be at 66th and California. Ground was broken at 68th and Washtenaw on July 4, 1928.

Early Marquette Manor residents Frank and Kate Hughes pose on the front steps of their home at 6308 South Campbell.

Marquette Manor resident Wm. Peter Dargis was the owner of the first Phillips 66 filling station in Chicago, opening the station in 1929, at 68th and Western. The station originally had four employees, but in only a few months, the staff increased to nine men working the pumps, lube, and pits. At times, the station had traffic backed up half a block down Western Avenue with cars waiting to get gas. This location soon became the Phillips 66 Company's number-one filling station in the country.

Rev. Anthony Staniukynas, while collecting donations for the Sisters' congregation, also requested donations for orphans. Looking out the window of the newly-built Motherhouse, he longed to see an orphanage built on the adjacent 10 acres. Cardinal Mundelein preferred land outside the city limits for an orphanage and the present land be used for a hospital instead. That plan was implemented, and on February 28, 1928, Holy Cross opened its doors.

Three

MARQUETTE PARK
PLAYGROUND OF THE
SOUTHWEST SIDE

The story of Marquette Park began in 1900, when the burgeoning development of Chicago Lawn threatened to take over all of the available land. Farms were disappearing as rows of houses sprouted up in their place. Realizing action needed to be taken quickly, the town forefathers appealed to the South Park commissioners, asking them to secure a public park for the Southwest Side. The general idea for the park was to have an area set aside for hunting, fishing, and boating.

The entire community came out for the gala opening of the 323-acre park on July 4, 1906. Yet, the actual building of the park took nearly a quarter of a century. Its nine-hole golf course, 3 1/2 miles of waterway winding around the grounds, and eight bridges connecting the islands of Marquette Park to the mainland have made it one of the more unique parks in the city. It stands now as a testament to the perseverance of John Eberhart and the early leaders of Chicago Lawn.

The Mossler farmhouse, sitting at approximately 68th and St. Louis, served as the first fieldhouse in the early days. The two-story frame was renovated, with the first floor serving as a combined headquarters and warming room for skaters. The upper floor was remodeled into a five-room apartment for the first foreman of the park, Edwin Eagle, his wife Augusta, and their son Clarence.

Edwin Eagle, pictured here on the steps of the fieldhouse, served as foreman of Marquette Park for the first 23 years. It has been said that rarely a movement was made by anyone in the park that didn't fall on the watchful eye of Eagle and his field glasses.

Among the first activities at the park were tobogganing and ice skating. Initially, the toboggan slide was located at what would be west of Kedzie at the south end of the park. After only a couple of years, a newer, higher one was built near the old Mossler house.

This early bandstand in Marquette Park was the site of concerts on many a warm summer night. Concert-goers sat on the ground surrounding this large gazebo. Posing on the bandstand for this picture were (left to right): Carl Welch, Kitty Delfeld, Harry Wilton, Clara Delfeld, Dane Noland, Edith Delfeld, and George Hewitt.

The golf course opened at Marquette Park in 1913. The first tee, pictured above, was located near 71st and Sacramento. The course was rearranged five times to provide improvements in the topographical beauty of the park and once to facilitate the extension of Kedzie Avenue through the center of the park. Finally in 1934, the layout of the course as we know it today was set in place.

Marquette Park has always been a popular destination for field trips. Pictured here in 1940 is Summer Story Hour at the park, featuring popular librarian Elizabeth King, in the center of the photo, from the Chicago Lawn Branch Public Library. Storyteller Rose Levenson, also from the Chicago Lawn Branch, is on the far right of the picture. Elizabeth King died in February 2000, at the age of 91.

A city-wide consolidation in 1934 put Marquette Park under the jurisdiction of the Chicago Park District. Shortly thereafter, the golf shelter, built in 1917, was remodeled into a fieldhouse. Now that Marquette was finally equipped with a gymnasium, auditorium, and clubrooms, a full agenda of park district activities could be offered. Pictured here are spectators at the Boxing Show held on May 20, 1938.

Open House Week at the fieldhouse included this dance on March 19, 1938.

The Chicago Lawn Girls' Baseball Team is pictured here in 1915. Team members were: (front row) H. Halvorsen, Bernice Heiser, Irene Meisney, Julia Clark, Florence Heiser; (center) Lilly Jones, Jean Travis; (back row) Helen Halvorsen, Carol Oakes, Thelma Maier, Florence Knup, Emma Helwig, Hazel Travis, and Mil Travis.

Marquette Park has long been a favorite fishing spot. The 3 1/2 miles of lagoon with eight bridges connecting the islands of Marquette Park make a beautiful and relaxing summer retreat. Anglers travel in from neighboring city and suburban communities to take advantage of the well-stocked waters.

The Therapeutic Recreation program at Marquette Park has long been considered one of the best in the city. For over 20 years, its members have brought home countless awards for their expertise in a variety of sports.

This snapshot taken on October 17, 1938, shows the Marquette Park Boys Softball Champions.

As the sign says, before the City of Chicago began holding the Fourth of July fireworks celebration off Navy Pier, Marquette Park had Chicago's largest fireworks display. You had to pack up your blanket and get there early if you wanted a good spot on the hill.

As the years went on, model rockets and planes began to join kites in the sky over Marquette Park.

Stretching from 67th to 71st Street and Central Park east to California, Marquette Park is so big that it has two playgrounds on opposite ends. A sandbox and a sprinkler accompany the playground in the northwest corner. In this 1980s picture, Abby Meyer is enjoying the new play equipment put in at the southeast corner.

Summertime means Day Camp at Chicago Parks. These Marquette Park Day Campers had just taken part in Police Day in 1980.

Early members of the Marquette Park Football Club pictured here were, from left to right: (kneeling/sitting) Elmer Wilton, Floyd Tully, Bill Renderer, Carl Wisemeyer, Herb Clarkson, Joe Wisemeyer, Myron Greene, Roy Lewis; (standing) Joe Wolfe, Lorin Smith, Don Stevenson, Walter Mumford, Ed Hock, and Harry Hirsch.

Once a year for 25 years, the Iroquois District of the Boy Scouts transformed Marquette Park into a huge Indian village. The annual powwows took place in June over Father's Day weekend. This particular powwow was in 1970.

On April 16, 1938, these kids were at an Easter Egg Hunt in Marquette Park. They filled their baskets with eggs hidden along the banks of the lagoon.

Could anyone have grown up in the vicinity of Marquette Park and not taken a turn sledding down the "big hill" at Sacramento? In this 1987 picture, Marta Ruikis posed on top of the hill with grandchildren Donna, Paul, and John.

Marquette Park provides a year-round home for flocks of ducks and geese as brothers Al, Val, and Ray Gencius found on a Thanksgiving Day stroll through the park in 1991. This picture was taken around the southeastern leg of the lagoon near 71st Street.

In March of 1971, this Marquette Park Girls Dance class put on a production entitled *Windy City Springtime*. Featured in the show was this tap specialty performed to "Raindrops Keep Falling on My Head."

This February 1939 picture shows a demonstration of Lithuanian folk dancing in the auditorium of the fieldhouse. Lithuanian dance instructor was Vytantas Belijaus, pictured at right.

Cleaning debris from the edges of the lagoon has been a never-ending battle throughout the years. Working on that project in September of 1974 are members of Cub Scout Pack 3620, sponsored by Thomas Memorial United Church of Christ: (left to right) Gary Krol, Denise Garrett, Denmother Mrs. Ann Gogue, David Valkenburg, Jerry Gogue Jr., Jerry Gogue Sr., and Ald John Madrzyk (13th).

Standing in the northeast corner of Marquette Park, the Darius-Girenus monument honors the memory and contains the epitaphs of two men who attempted to forge an intangible and unbreakable link between a beloved old country and a beloved new one. In 1999, the Lithuanian-American community spearheaded a campaign to refurbish the monument. Albertas Kerelis Jr. spoke at the rededication ceremony, which was held on the 66th anniversary of the transatlantic flight.

And in the northwest corner of Marquette Park stands this monument dedicated to men of a much earlier time. It reads: THIS TABLET AND ADJACENT ELM TREE STAND HERE AS A MEMORIAL TO THOSE FROM THIS COMMUNITY WHO SERVED IN THE WORLD WAR 1914–1918.

Four

GROWTH OF TWO
NEIGHBORHOODS

Both of the neighborhoods surrounding Marquette Park experienced substantial growth at the end of the First World War. The community of Marquette Manor was coming into its own and growing westward, as Chicago Lawn edged eastward. Gradually the two neighborhoods were merging together.

Just three decades earlier, Kedzie was considered the outskirts of town. By 1938, when this picture was taken, that was certainly not the case. Looking north on Kedzie from atop the Marquette Theater Building, retail development was filling in the once-empty prairies. Houses now spread out north, south, east, and west of Kedzie as more and more lots were subdivided; 59th Street, 69th Street, and 71st Street were now joining 63rd Street as major centers of activity in the community.

Development halted with the onset of World War II, as the community waited for news from the front. But there was really nothing left to build. The two neighborhoods now offered most any amenities. For the most part, new developmental influences in the next few decades would come from outside the community borders.

Thanks to the efforts of the Chicago Lawn Women's Club, the area received its first official branch of the Chicago Public Library. Located on the southwest corner of 62nd Place and Kedzie, it replaced the original community library housed on about a half-dozen bookshelves in the rear of Hagerman's Dry Goods store.

In 1925, the community's rapid growth brought plans for a million-dollar show house. Built on the northwest corner of 59th and Kedzie, the Colony had a seating capacity of 2,500. Destined to become one of the largest showplaces of its time, the Colony Theatre opened in autumn of that year. In the 1990s, a segment of the Early Edition television show was filmed at the Colony.

The old two-story frame firehouse that served as a gathering place for the early Chicago Lawn fathers burned beyond repair in the summer of 1914. This brick station built on the same spot became the new home of Engine Co. 88. In this photo, firemen pose outside for the camera in 1938.

This 1938 view looking east from the Grand Trunk tracks shows 63rd Street becoming a shopping center and filling in quite nicely. Parking is already getting a little tighter. Notice the Shell filling station on the right selling 9 gallons of gas for $1. The tavern on the north side of the street is advertising Edelweiss beer, and the one across the street advertises Monarch beer.

Looking east on 63rd Street in 1938, this photo was taken from the top of the Troy Lane Hotel. Father and Son Shoes and the United Liquors sign are visible on the left of the picture. F.W. Woolworth is just west of United. The sign for Shaller Appliances hangs over the building on the northeast corner of 63rd and Albany.

The Lawn Club Hall, once a favorite gathering place of local groups, was destroyed by fire and subsequently torn down to make way for a much-needed parking lot for the police station next door. As the picture shows, the last business to occupy the front store was Charles Barber Shop.

The huge Marzano's Million Dollar "Palace of Pleasure," stretching from 3315 to 3331 on 63rd Street, urged residents to "keep in step with the rhythm and pep of the Marquette Entertainers," who were scheduled to perform at the grand opening dance in January of 1931. Admission was 50¢.

Albert Berg moved to Marquette Manor in 1906, and became one of the community's first paint contractors. In 1947, sons Ernest, Albert, and Edwin joined their father in opening this retail paint and wallpaper store on the northeast corner of 63rd and Rockwell.

In 1936, Polyhronis (Paul) Stefanos rented a storefront at 79th and Ashland next to the Highland Theatre, selling popcorn for 5¢. He and his wife Pauline made toffee and fudge in the back room. In 1946, they opened the Cupid Candies location at 3143 West 63rd Street that would grow into the candy and ice cream shop best remembered by a generation of Southwest Siders. Paul is pictured above in this store in 1956. Jane Kaminski is behind the counter.

When Burton's Store for Men closed up shop, Mr. Steer Steakhouse moved in next to Cupid Candies. Just a hop, skip, and a jump from the Marquette Theatre, the three made a great combination for a Saturday night out on 63rd Street.

The Illinois Billiard Club began in the home of James Parker at 64th and Artesian. Later at its 71st Street location, Hollywood came to IBC, launching a marketing campaign promoting the movie *Baltimore Bullet* and a national live tournament held at the club. Director Martin Scorsese followed, bringing Paul Newman and Tom Cruise to IBC to learn the sport and film *The Color of Money*. The club was named number one out of 150 "Best of the Best" by *Chicago Magazine* in the commemorative issue of the city's 150th anniversary.

In March of 1971, a smiling Richard Friedman, Republican candidate for mayor, took a walk through the Southwest Side with State Rep. Walter "Babe" McAvoy (27th) and Ald. Casimir Stazcuk, candidate for re-election in the 13th Ward. The Southwest News-Herald office building in the background was built in 1950, and at that time was one of the most modern community newspaper offices in the country, designed to be an asset to the community.

Eight progressive merchants pose with eight portable television sets they gave away in a "Prize of the Month" contest. Left to right are: Joseph Nathan of Nathan's Style Shop, John Kitsos of General TV and Electronics, James Angone of ABC Dinette Co., Stuart Zemsky of Zemsky's Fashions, Harry Scheck of ABC Sewing Machine Co., John Hunt of Hunt Jewelers, George Slater of Slater's Shoes, and Joseph Herbert of Marquette Photo Supply.

On the southeastern edge of Marquette Manor at 74th Street sits General Foods. For many years, the nation's Kool-Aid was made right here. This picture, taken on January 8, 1952, shows a happy birthday toast by employees. And, believe it or not, their cups are filled with Kool-Aid.

One of the many popular eateries throughout the years was Little Joe's on 63rd Street. Famous across the Southwest Side for both Italian and American cuisine, Little Joe's also offered entertainment on the weekends in the form of pop vocalist and guitarist Aldo.

Ed Vondrak, publisher of the *Southwest News-Herald* (far left) joined local dignitaries as parking meters were adjusted along Kedzie Avenue in 1964. Vondrak had requested an increase in time to allow for leisurely shopping in the community. In the background, the former home of the Chicago Lawn Branch Library is now JoSelle's Bridal Fashions. And Republic Savings, founded by John J. Jilek in 1933, had moved to this Kedzie location in the 1950s.

In the 1920s and 1930s, the Chicago Bungalow joined the early farmhouses in landscaping the neighborhood blocks. Both Chicago Lawn and Marquette Manor are members in good standing of the Bungalow Belt. Here St. Nicholas of Tolentine Catholic Church looks down on one of the many rows of Chicago Bungalows scattered throughout both communities.

As this early picture of houses in the process of construction on the 3500 block of West 65th demonstrates, Chicago Lawn is not limited to bungalows.

Vintage well-cared-for homes such as this one are prominent in Chicago Lawn. Traffic slows down in front of this particular one on the northeast corner of 64th and Lawndale to get a glimpse of the seasonal decorations always displayed on the front porch.

While Marquette Manor has its share of bungalows, the slightly newer community also has many unique homes such as this one on California Avenue. Distinct construction can be found up and down neighborhood streets.

For many years, the Christmas shopping season began when Santa arrived in the 63rd and Kedzie shopping area, joined in the community parade, and later played host at the annual giant theater party sponsored by the Chicago Lawn Chamber of Commerce. The Marquette Manor Businessmen's Association held their own Christmas theater party at the Hi-Way Theatre.

Mike Trost is pictured here inside the family-owned business at 3111 West 63rd. The popular hobby shop actually began as a hardware store. Mike's parents moved their store to its Chicago Lawn location from 37th and Halsted in 1923. In 1928, his mother bought a few airplane kits, put them in a showcase, and their hobby business began, eventually expanding to include three more storefronts. Also pictured is manager Ed Transier.

Ford City opened its doors in August of 1965, bringing 82 new stores just outside the backyard of Chicago Lawn. Located just 15 minutes away, Ford City was Chicago's first enclosed air-conditioned shopping center and advertised as a shopper's paradise. Early tenants included National Tea, Allison's Apparel, Andes Candies, Flagg Bros., Tally-Ho Snack Shop, and Harvest House Cafeteria. In this picture, shoppers take advantage of one of the many sidewalk sales.

The *Chicago Tribune* reported: "Open the door and walk into what could be the cocktail lounge of a ski resort in Colorado. Knight's Inn is most popular in winter when the fireplace is roaring and the illusion of being in the mountains is strongest." Originally a bank building, the vault was converted into the kitchen. Works of local artists lined one wall, and there were parties for every occasion in this popular club on Lithuanian Plaza Court.

On January 26 and 27, the great snowfall of 1967 paralyzed Chicago. While the storm left thousands stranded, the police had to be inventive. Chicago Lawn police borrowed a toboggan from a neighbor to get an expectant mother to Holy Cross Hospital. They used a sled to transport a heart attack victim the three blocks to Holy Cross. This is how the 6600 block of Mozart looked after the snowfall.

Once the plows were able to begin clearing the streets, it was possible to venture out a little further from home. In this shot, taken from California Avenue looking north, two well-known establishments on the corner of 63rd and California peek out from behind the snow—Jarek Drugs and Leader Cleaners.

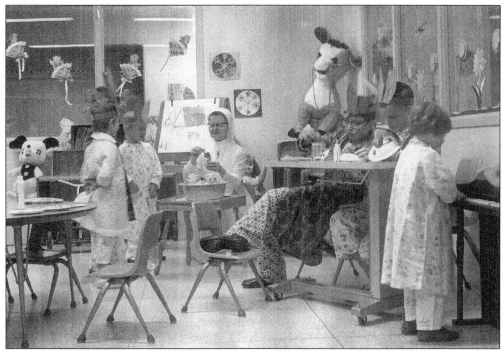

In 1956, Holy Cross Hospital was running at capacity, placing beds on sun porches and every other available space to meet demand, but non-emergency patients often went several weeks before gaining admittance. The Sisters of St. Casimir, who staffed the hospital, addressed the problem by announcing a $4,000,000 expansion project. The hospital has continued expanding through the years. This picture from the late 1960s shows Sister Francine in the pediatrics ward.

In 1964, the new Southwest Expressway, which would make travel a lot easier for Southwest Side residents, was under construction. This picture looks west from the Ashland Avenue construction phase. The Southwest Council of Civic Organizations urged the Cook County Board to rename the road MacArthur Expressway after the famous general who led the armed forces in the Southwest Pacific during World War II. We know the road today as the Stevenson Expressway.

In November of 1970, the northwest corner of 63rd and California was leveled as five stores and apartments above were demolished to make way for a new three-bay gas station. On the south side of the street is Yanas Hardware, and on the corner of 63rd and Mozart is the Gaspipe Club.

In the late 1960s, Chicken Unlimited was a fast food staple in many Chicago neighborhoods, advertising chicken "Tender as quail and Tasty as pheasant." The original franchise unit, pictured here, opened in 1965 at 6250 South Kedzie. The owner, Sam Simone, was a graduate of St. Rita High School. Members of his staff included Mrs. Gerry Lopac, day manager; and Mrs. Gert Shimkus, night manager.

As anyone in the vicinity could tell you, the Gold Coast Inn at 2525 West 71st Street had great Fish Frys on Friday night. Among its many other celebrations, the restaurant was the site of Rev. Francis X. Lawlor's victory party when, running as an Independent, he snagged the 15th Ward Aldermanic seat from incumbent Paul M. Sheridan. At the time, Gold Coast's host was Joe Rachunas. Later it would be the Laurians.

Passers-by posed for the camera after checking out the damaged police car in this late 1960s photo taken at 63rd and Francisco. In the background is King's Drive-In, a popular after school stopping place. When this picture was taken, malts were 25¢, a chicken dinner was $1.35, and 21 pieces of shrimp were 99¢.

Gertie's Ice Cream Parlor on the corner of 59th and Kedzie was a favorite of young and old alike for many decades.

If a dentist was needed, John J. Simkus, DDS had his office on 63rd and Western above Marquette Bank. When the bank needed his space, Simkus moved to 63rd Street, right across from St. Rita. He's sitting here in front of his home on 70th and California. Orphaned at the age of six, he and his brother and sister were taken in by his 18-year-old aunt who raised them, and incidentally built this house.

The 63rd Street Art Fair, held in June, displayed works of art from Albany to Homan. This 1971 shot was taken right outside the National Food Store.

Across the street and down the block from Gertie's sat Yankee Doodle Dandy. When the chain closed its stores in Chicago in the 1980s, the building became the home of T.J. Michaels Restaurant.

This 1950s aerial view was taken to show the institutions of the Sisters of St. Casimir. It also reflects the growth of a neighborhood.

Five

CHURCHES AND
SCHOOLS

The roots and the growth of Marquette Manor were embedded in religion and education. So too were the spiritual and educational needs of the people of utmost importance to John Eberhart in Chicago Lawn. The first school and the first church services were held in the parlor of Eberhart's home. As the tiny settlement grew, the train depot became the new meeting place, followed by Lawn Club Hall.

Rev. Alexander Monroe, pictured here, came to Chicago Lawn in 1902, and became the first minister of the Chicago Lawn Congregational Church. He was 6 foot 3 inches tall and when seen walking across the prairies on a call to an absent member, it was said he reminded one of Abraham Lincoln.

Many congregations have called Chicago Lawn and Marquette Manor their home. This chapter celebrates the largest and those that have endured the longest. The remarkable growth and vigor of these congregations is characteristic of the development of the Southwest Side of Chicago.

C.H. Lyon's Real Estate office, pictured here at 5931 South Kedzie, was the original meeting place of Grace Church. In 1921, the little congregation had nine members. By 1923, it had grown to 125 and needed a larger place to worship.

St. Elizabeth Episcopal Church was founded in November 1903, when Rev. William C. Way conducted the first service in the Lawn Club building. A little more than a year later, the congregation purchased three lots on the southwest corner of 62nd and St. Louis. The present church, pictured here, was completed in 1908, and then remodeled in 1921 to provide space for an auditorium and kitchen.

The Nazareth congregation, organized in 1917, erected their first church, a portable chapel, on the corner of 60th and Hamlin in 1919. After canvassing the neighborhood, it became evident the chapel was not in the most advantageous spot and should relocate closer to Kedzie. This picture, taken May 12, 1928, shows the church-member Grounds Clean-up Crew on the day before dedication ceremonies of Nazareth Ev. Lutheran Church at 60th and Spaulding.

After only one year in their storefront church, the Hope Lutheran congregation filled the building to capacity. The site at 64th and Washtenaw was purchased, and the cornerstone of the first unit was laid in 1918. Before long, rapid growth compelled the congregation to again devise a plan for larger quarters. On August 6, 1922, the plans became a reality, and this new church was dedicated.

The Eberhart School at 65th Place and Homan Avenue is the oldest school in Chicago Lawn. The current edifice was built in 1911 at a cost of $190,000, and has since been remodeled many times over. Originally known as the Chicago Lawn School, its first classes were held back in 1876, in the parlor of John Eberhart's home. Upon Eberhart's death in 1914, the school's name was changed to honor the "Father of Chicago Lawn."

The Chicago Lawn Presbyterian Church was organized on May 17, 1908, in the K.P. Hall on the northeast corner of 63rd and St. Louis with 60 charter members. On January 1, 1911, the organization moved into its own new building, pictured here, at 62nd and St. Louis.

In September 1915, Mr. Ira Baker, then principal of Earle School and a pioneer of Marquette Manor, petitioned the Board of Education to build a portable school in the Manor. The site selected was the northwest corner of 61st and Maplewood. As enrollment grew, more portables were added. Finally in 1925, the portables were vacated, and a new building was opened at 60th and Rockwell and christened the Donald L. Morrill School.

On June 8, 1928, George Cardinal Mundelein appointed Rev. Leo McNamara to establish St. Adrian parish. McNamara was to organize English-speaking Catholics who lived south of St. Rita. Sunday Masses were celebrated at McKay Public School until completion of this Tudor Gothic on the southwest corner of 70th and Washtenaw in September 1929.

The Palm Sunday choir of the Chicago Lawn Presbyterian Church posed for this picture in 1955.

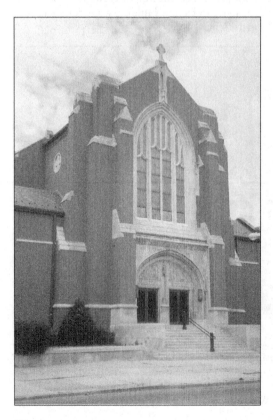

While Marquette Manor is home to three Catholic parishes, Chicago Lawn has not one. St. Nicholas of Tolentine Church sits on the western boundary and was established as a mission church of St. Rita in 1909, and put under the pastoral care of Rev. Charles O'Neill, a faculty member at St. Rita College. Father O'Neill found about 170 Catholics in the area around the mission.

In 1927, the Parent-Teachers Association of Marquette Grade School was appealing to the Chicago Board of Education to increase its planned addition. The school was to move into a new eight-room wing in January 1928. However, acting superintendent William Bogan felt that relief to the overcrowding would come in the form of the new Francis McKay School pictured here at 68th and Washtenaw.

These members of the Grace Church Council met to discuss plans for a new church in 1927.

ST. ADRIAN CLASS 1931

In 1929, St. Adrian Grammar School opened under the direction of the religious order commonly known as the Ladies of Loretto. The picture above is the first graduating class in 1931. With the many new homes being built in the area, enrollment increased rapidly. In 1951, attention was given to the extreme overcrowding. An addition known as the Little School was completed in October of 1953.

Standing on the northwest corner of 69th and Washtenaw, Nativity BVM Catholic Church was established on May 15, 1927, as a Lithuanian National Parish by Rev. Alexander Baltutis and a lay committee of 15. Originally a church/school Tudor Gothic, the church quarters were remodeled into a gym when this new edifice was completed in 1957. Features incorporating Lithuanian folk architecture and Baroque design give the building a distinctive Lithuanian motif.

The privately run Lithuanian Montessori Preschool was at 69th and Fairfield, right across from Holy Cross Hospital. Classes were taught in the Lithuanian language. By the late 1970s and 1980s, many of the parents sending their children to the school had been students there themselves many years before. Pictured here in October of 1981 are Donna, age four and a half, and Paul, age three, Gencius.

The photographer got these members of the St. Rita of Cascia kindergarten class to smile for the camera in 1956.

Mrs. Sarah Alden taught this kindergarten class at Eberhart School. She guesses this photo to be the class of 1943.

Thomas Memorial Congregational Church grew out of the Chicago Lawn Union Church, which started as a mission in 1897. The first church, pictured here, was erected in 1902 on 62nd Place near St. Louis. The congregation outgrew this church almost as soon as it was dedicated. The building was remodeled into an apartment house when the congregation moved out.

The Lawn Manor Hebrew Congregation was founded by Jewish immigrants from Eastern Europe in a loft on 63rd Street. Members built this stone synagogue at 66th and Troy in 1925. As the membership grew in the 1950s, the congregation built a new synagogue and community center at 66th and Kedzie. This building is now home to the Lithuanian Evangelical Lutheran Church.

Under the direction of the Sisters of St. Dominic of Adrian, Michigan, St. Nicholas of Tolentine School opened its doors on September 12, 1910. The little four-room schoolhouse was located above the church. Two rooms were used as classrooms and two for the Sisters' living quarters. Tuition was 50¢. This photo shows the student body in 1911.

Construction on the present St. Rita Church began in 1948. The largest on the Southwest Side, it represented a feat in engineering as it was built right around the old building without any interruption of services. New walls were erected around the outside, and the old ones were removed later. Dedication took place on the golden jubilee of the canonization of St. Rita of Cascia, patroness of the parish.

The 69-year history of St. Adrian Grammar School came to a close when these 13 graduates received their diplomas in 1998. With public school enrollment increasing dramatically and Catholic school enrollment declining, the Little School was leased to the Chicago Public School system, and the original school was transformed into the Marquette Development Center. This new venture serves as a job training center that works closely with companies in the area matching employers with prospective employees.

In 1921, early settlers established the Marquette Manor Baptist Church, holding services at the Marquette Clubhouse on 60th and Fairfield until 1923, when the growing membership moved into a bungalow church at 59th and Rockwell. The church building at 60th and California was erected in 1931, and an educational building added in 1951. In 1971, Marquette Manor Baptist celebrated its 50th anniversary, but before another decade passed, fire would leave the church in ruins.

EBERHART SCHOOL   PATROL BOYS   MARCH 1950

These smiling young gentlemen were patrol boys at Eberhart School in 1950.

In 1971, Miss Joan Lapa, a student teacher at Marquette Elementary School, asked her third graders to write letters to State Sen. Frank D. Savickas requesting that he support anti-pollution legislation. In this picture taken on Monday morning, the 18th of November, the students are hard at work on their assignment.

As with St. Nicholas of Tolentine, Hubbard High School sits just outside the border of Chicago Lawn. Originally built as an elementary school, the two-story building consisted of two rooms on the first floor and two on the second, with a back balcony used as the principal's office. The flagpole was located in the middle of the building and whenever the flag was raised, a second-floor window had to be opened.

When Thomas Memorial Congregational Church outgrew its original worship space, the cornerstone for this edifice was laid in September 1913, on land donated by Mrs. Hiriam W. Thomas. Until 1999, this building at 64th Place and Homan housed the oldest congregation in Chicago Lawn and Marquette Manor.

The St. Rita parish choir posed in front of the church with choir director Don Peterson and organist Mary Sublewski in July 1993.

St. Rita High School introduced a technical department in 1936, offering courses in woodshop, metal shop, shop drafting, and eventually electricity, radio, and aeronautics.

From 1942 to 1952, Rev. John Fitzgerald was the aeronautics instructor at St. Rita. In the rear of the Tech building was a 50' by 50' room known as "The Hangar." Fr. Fitzgerald would bring in real planes by trailer and do some repair work on them with his students. From time to time, he would take them flying at Ashburn Flying Field on 83rd and Cicero.

In the early days, St. Casimir Academy was both a day and boarding school for girls. Although founded primarily for the education of girls of Lithuanian descent, the school extended a cordial welcome to girls of other nationalities as well.

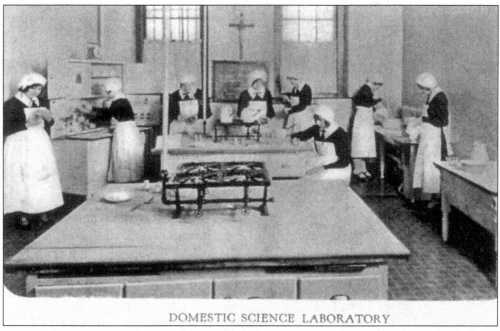

DOMESTIC SCIENCE LABORATORY

St. Casimir Academy offered eight different courses of education. The girls in this photo took advantage of the four-year Household course and are working in what was then the new and fully-equipped Domestic Science Laboratory.

The Children's Choir of Nazareth Lutheran Church posed for this picture with their choir director, William F. Wittmer, in 1942.

This historic building, which sat on the corner of 63rd Place and St. Louis, once housed the first church established in Chicago Lawn. Built in 1890, the First Methodist Church celebrated its 55th anniversary in May 1947, by burning their mortgage. Early the following Thanksgiving morning, its congregation watched as the church, engulfed in flames, burned to the ground. Plans to rebuild took four years to fulfill.

Members of the St. Rita Grammar School Class of 1994 posed for this picture shortly before their graduation in May. Upon their graduation they would become the last graduating class in the grammar school's 79-year history. The first Catholic grammar school built in Chicago Lawn or Marquette Manor would not re-open in 1995. The parish leases the building to the Chicago Public Schools, and it is now home to Fairfield Academy.

110 A.M. KDG.   MARQUETTE SCHOOL   MARCH 1978

The morning kindergarten class of Marquette School is pictured here in March of 1978. The school opened its doors in September 1926, with an enrollment of 1,080 pupils. Twenty-four rooms were needed to accommodate the children. The predominant nationalities of the pupils were listed as German and Lithuanian.

Students that were a part of the Lithuanian Song Festival posed outside of Nativity BVM on June 30, 1957.

Members of the Vacation Bible School at Hope Lutheran Church posed for this photo in front of the church in 1954.

St. Elizabeth's Choir Boys processed into church in 1931. They are, from left to right: John Silvis, Robert Lisk, Carl Larson, James Smith, Samuel Neve Jr., George Silvis, Ralph Connor, James Parliman, Joseph Parliman, David Logan Jr., and Charles Skerritt.

Sister Marietta of the Sisters of St. Casimir was an art teacher as well as an elementary education teacher at Nativity BVM. Sister specialized in wood carvings, and one in particular hangs at Holy Cross Hospital. On the right side of the picture is Sister Emmanuel, who later become principal of Nativity.

This May Crowning picture at St. Rita of Cascia shows the eighth graders chosen as the court to process in and crown the Virgin Mary. Pictured on the right is eighth grader Anne McGlone. She is now Illinois Appellate Court Justice Anne Burke, and among her other accomplishments she has received much recognition for her work as one of the founders of the Special Olympics.

In 1942, 54 staff and board members of Nazareth Ev. Lutheran Church, all community residents, comprised the 25th anniversary committee of the church. Two more additions, built in 1949 and 1960, added a grade school, church offices, and social rooms.

Here members of the Lawn Manor Beth Jacob Congregation get together for one of the many ice cream socials in the '70s and '80s put on by the Sisterhood. In 1973, the Beth Jacob Congregation from the Scottsdale neighborhood merged with Lawn Manor. For many decades now, the Lawn Manor Beth Jacob Congregation has been the only remaining synagogue on the Southwest Side.

For over 30 years, the SSC Motherhouse also served as a novitiate and the St. Casimir Academy for girls. When the halls could no longer hold the growing enrollment, the Academy set its site on the land directly west of its building. The newly expanded school, which opened on September 8, 1952, was christened Maria High School.

Six

SOCIAL LIVES OF THE LAWN AND MANOR

In the earliest days, there were no cars, radios, or movies, so the pioneers were left to their own resources for entertainment. The first regular social activity on record was the watermelon feast. A notice tacked up in the train depot announced a party would be held at a certain home on a certain night, and that was all that was necessary. Everyone who wanted to come was invited. The feast pictured above shows the Schlieske children enjoying their watermelon at a Labor Day party in their backyard.

The first social club on record was the Literary Club. Members met at each other's homes to read the town newspaper. Only one copy, usually written in pen and ink, was published and it had to be passed around. So if one missed the meeting, he may have to wait a month or more before the newspaper made it to his house.

By the early 1900s, sports teams, men's and women's clubs, a Masonic lodge, and a Boy Scout troop had been formed. Plays, ball games, parades, and concerts were now a regular part of the social lives of the people.

This picture was given to Charlie Sherman as a Christmas gift in 1910, from Joyce Weston. The Shermans lived at 3629 West 64th Street. Pictured here are: (top row) L. Westenfelter, F. Ryan, George Weston, Charles Ash; (bottom row) August Schlieske, Franklin Smith, Ted Britton, Dave Trumbull, George Vivian, and Charlie Sherman.

Otandalu Campfire Girls present The Chicago Lawn Library a copy of their new Campfire manual. Photographed by

The Otandalu Campfire Girls of Chicago Lawn visited the Chicago Lawn Branch Library to present them with a copy of their new Campfire manual.

The Chicago Lawn Methodist Church took first place in the Church League in 1938. Pictured here with their trophies are: (back row) Richard Halstrom, N. Stewart, Felix Janchas, Edgar Jacot, Robert Malone, Robert Gibson, Henry Polson; (front row) Harry Jarn, Edward Jandecek, Unidentified, Rev. Stocton Swaney, Gael MacDonald, and William Kulling.

Hazel Wood, born and raised in Chicago Lawn, was called "the girl with the golden voice" by the director of the Chicago Grand Opera Company. She received rave reviews from drama critic Charles Nixon for her portrayal of a prima donna while touring with the Pantages Circuit during the 1915–16 season. Miss Wood is pictured at right while playing in *The Little Lost Sister* during the winter of 1913–14.

St. Rita High School named their football field after legendary coach Pat Cronin (third from the left). Standing with Cronin are halfback Billy Marek and Lineman Dennis Lick, who both went on to become starring players at the University of Wisconsin. West Lawn resident Dennis Lick, of course, also went on to play for the Chicago Bears. This 1972 team went on to win the city championship.

In 1958, the dream of a neighborhood pool was alive and well. On January 15, Anthony Duvall, newly-elected chairman of the West Communities YMCA board, announced that the goal of the organization for 1958 would be the erection of a swimming pool as an addition to their building at 6235 South Homan. The campaign to raise $76,500 was realized, giving thousands of children as these a place to swim.

Performing as a Ritanette during half-time at a St. Rita High School football game is the future Honorable Anne M. Burke, Illinois Appellate Court Justice. So pleased was she with the education she received at Maria High School, Mrs. Burke and her husband, Alderman Edward M. Burke (14th), founded the Anne McGlone Burke Scholarship awarded annually to promising Maria High School students.

Robert Robertson, Theodora Skwer, Mona Amato, and Philip Broman pose for a picture while singing Christmas carols at the old Chicago Lawn Branch Library on 62nd and Kedzie in December of 1946.

The "Sewing Circle Club" poses for a picture at the home of Mrs. R.L. Williams in the spring of 1911. Pictured here are: (standing) Florence Irving, Bessie Seward, Abbie Wilcox, Inez Stoneman; (seated) Nettie Seward, Mabelle Carr, Grace Hampton, Helen Bursmith, and Nellie Irving.

Here are the Chicago Lawn Girl Scouts in 1939. Pictured are: (bottom) Vivian Dolay, Audrey LeSeur, Carol Hood, Marjorie Padrta, Shirley Crane, Alice Martz, Ruth Ashcroft, Elizabeth Hill; (second) Patricia Nielsen, Florence Norton, Marian Ruckel, Hazel Schoondermark, Bonnie Jean Padrta, Eileen Rossow, Ethel Cooley, Mary Prat, Vilma Ward; (third) Zilla Norton, Patricia Wilson, Lois Maxfield, Norma Gilbert, Betty Hacker, Elaine Manchen; (top) Marion Nielsen, Collete Gerard, Jeanne Malone, Dorothy Price, Ruth Fries, Janet Norhelfer, Patricia Pratt, Jean Nielsen, Dorothy Scanlon, June Wilke, Lorraine Tanka (leaders) Jean LeSeur, Velma Leiferman, and Lorraine Collins.

Actors in one of the many plays put on by the Marquette Manor Club include: Frances Briody, Ernest Coyle, Unidentified, Harold Fax, ? Melander, Unidentified, Agnes Zeder, Fred Rumpf, Joseph Rogers, Mrs. E. Coyle, Unidentified, and Frank Northrup. This photo was taken in 1917.

Baby Doll Parties were popular in the early 1900s; this one was held in 1912, at the Travis home. Pictured are: (front) Julie Clark Keile, Irma Tucker, Kathleen McNally Peters, Martha Ashby Smith, Alma Plant; (center, seated) Unidentified, Helen Halvorsen Gustafson, Florence Knup Conn, Vivien Stenmark, Mildred Travis, Marie Martins; (standing) Irene Misner Peters, Marie Mortell, Hazel Ashy Rapp, Helen Westenfelder Small, Carol Oakes Beach, Alberta Brown, Unidentified, Hazel Travis Umlor, Jean Travis Hanna, and Unidentified.

During the years of the Vietnam War, the Green Berets held a demonstration at the St. Rita Knights of Columbus Hall then located on 59th Street.

State Senator Frank Savickas presented this softball team from Clyde's Tavern with their winning trophy in front of his Marquette Manor office. Savickas was the first Lithuanian to hold this position.

The officers of the Marquette Manor Women's Club get ready to celebrate the 50th anniversary of the club's founding.

Ready for the city championship are these Morrill playground softball players and their phys-ed teacher Miss Esther Bergman.

The Sisters of St. Casimir Summerfest, a neighborhood tradition held annually on the second Sunday in July, always drew people from far and wide. Buses would begin arriving early with eager festival goers anxious to partake in the events of the day. This picture also suggests memories of the 69th Street Lithuanian Festival, begun in 1980. The streets filled with music, folk dancing, and the aroma of tasty Lithuanian cuisine.

Rev. John Kuziuskas, pastor of Nativity BVM and pictured here on the steps of the church, extended a hearty welcome to the President of Lithuania, Valdas Adamkus, and Mrs. Alma Adamkus during their visit to the United States.

Story Hour has always been quite popular at the Chicago Lawn Branch Library. This picture was taken after Story Hour on December 27, 1941.

Dennis Klima, president of the Chicago Lawn Chamber of Commerce and owner of Mid-State Beauty School on 63rd Street, congratulates members of the Hubbard High School baseball team on their 1973 state baseball championship win.

The annual procession and celebration of the Feast of Our Lady of Siluva is a time-honored tradition in the Lithuanian community. These ladies, dressed in native costume along with members of the Knights of Lithuania, led the procession in the year 2000, carrying the statue down the streets of the neighborhood.

The annual 63rd Street Holiday Parade takes place on the Saturday after Thanksgiving. Organized by the 63rd Street Growth Commission, a division of Greater Southwest Development Corporation, it is the largest community parade in Chicago. Pictured here in the year 1999 is the Hubbard High School Band marching east on the parade route past St. Rita of Cascia Catholic Church.

Seven

CHANGING TIMES AND VISION

By the later quarter of the 20th century, Chicago Lawn was getting ready to celebrate its 100th birthday, and Marquette Manor was not too far behind. Times were changing along with the needs of the people; 63rd Street had seen some changes as old-time stores were replaced with new ones. The once oft-frequented Marzano's Palace of Pleasure was torn down. Just as Flynn's Hall and the Lawn Theatre before it, Marzano's heyday was over. Developmental changes would now come to the community in the form of rehabs, senior housing complexes, and new shopping experiences.

Beginning in the late 1960s, Marquette Park, once known as the playground of the Southwest Side, had become a battleground. Panic peddling, blockbusting, and redlining, along with rallies, protests, and marches, put the community in a state of unrest. Groups from outside of the community picked Marquette Park as their demonstration ground and turned the once-complacent community into a news event.

However, by the 1990s, Chicago Lawn and Marquette Manor were making the news for other reasons. Pictured above are cameramen recording a Southwest Organizing Project event in 2001.

The proposed Crosstown Expressway threatened to displace homes in several Chicago neighborhoods, including Marquette Manor. Civic organizations formed a Common Council to address the issue. In May 1969, delegates from that council traveled to Washington, D.C. to meet with federal officials. From the bottom up are: Ald. Casimir Staszcuk (13th), Lawrence Hickey, Joseph Bacevicius, Robert Raczynski, Louis Dokas, Edward Jonish, John Ellias, Louis Marolda, Henry Coppolillo, and Irene Pisha.

Taking a stand against unscrupulous real estate practices prevalent in the '60s and '70s, the Marquette Park Lithuanian Homeowners Association marched through Marquette Park with signs reading "Panic Peddlers—Get Out," and "Don't Call Us, We'll Call You." Organized in 1937, the association serves to unite Lithuanian homeowners of the Marquette Park area in promoting order, cleanliness, and security for the community.

Rev. Francis X. Lawlor OSA gained notoriety for his community advocacy while holding the position of executive secretary of the Associated Block Clubs in the late 1960s. Hundreds of Lawlor supporters gathered to cheer the winner as he soundly defeated the incumbent in a race for the 15th Ward aldermanic seat. Lawlor is pictured here at his victory press conference.

Evidence of Lawlor's popularity as a strong leader for community stability is seen here as this packed auditorium listens while he and other community leaders address the heaviest issues weighing on the neighborhood at the time. Members of the audience hold signs reading "Stop the Blockbusting."

Civil rights groups marched west toward Marquette Park as the American Nazi Party, often accompanied by the Ku Klux Klan, marched east through the park to meet them. From 1966 to 1988, these marches took place on sporadic Sunday afternoons turning the bedroom community into a media stage.

After the first march in 1966, the American Nazi Party set up headquarters in the area. Police lined the major streets and arteries. Helicopters circled overhead as major news stations followed the events. Residents were encouraged to stay indoors or leave the neighborhood for the day. The demonstrations resulted in rock throwing, sometimes broken windows and injuries, and always arrests. Twenty-three arrests were made during the last march, 22 of those arrested were from outside the community. But the effect they had on the residents of the Marquette Park area was devastating.

Residents were appalled by the aftermath in the wake of these demonstrations. Some, like Acie Aydeolte of Chicago Lawn, took it upon themselves to erase the physical signs. Aydeolte, who deemed the graffiti disrespectful to the memory of aviators Captain Stephan Darius and Stanley Girenus, used paint thinner to remove markings from the monument. Broken tree limbs and litter would be cleaned from the park. Though the desecration was no more, the memory would live on.

The Southwest Community Congress stressed the right to peace in the community, seeking to prevent marches by Nazis and counter-demonstrators who were using Marquette Park as a stage for media events. They organized a petition drive against a proposed Klan rally at the park and joined the Religious Coalition to End Racial Violence in this Covenant Walk, holding services at St. Adrian Church and then marching to a proposed Klan demonstration site.

As the marches continued, Chicago Lawn and Marquette Manor had other projects to attend to. The first accomplishment of the Southwest Community Congress, founded in 1969, was to secure a site for a community college. Here Mayor Richard J. Daley presides at groundbreaking ceremonies for the institute of higher learning, which would later bear his name.

Chicago Lawn and Marquette Manor are a part of the Southwest Home Equity Assurance district. Disgusted with unscrupulous real estate practices in the 1960s and '70s, the community joined neighboring communities and, with the leadership of the Southwest Parish and Neighborhood Federation, devised the program. Several years in the making, residents, for the first time in the city's history, voted in a self-imposed tax for a program that guaranteed the value of their homes.

120

At this 1978 groundbreaking ceremony for the 63rd and Western beautification project, Mayor Michael Bilandic expressed enthusiasm for the project saying, "It was always an exciting experience to shop here with my parents when I was a child." Raising the ceremonial shovels are State Rep. Michael Madigan, Bilandic, and Henry Brozek. Supporting the effort are community representatives, supporters, and elected officials, including Jim Capraro, executive director of Greater Southwest Development Corp.

Greater Southwest Development Corporation was established in 1974. Enhancements to the community at the hands of GSDC, especially its main corridor 63rd Street, are much too numerous to list here. The above building, sitting prominently on the northeast corner of 63rd and Western was their first project. Neglected for years, it became an eyesore and an embarrassment to Marquette Manor. The newly-rehabbed building as it appears here was ready for occupancy in 1977.

Balzekas Museum of Lithuanian Culture opened in 1966, in the Brighton Park neighborhood. In 1986, Stanley Balzekas Jr., pictured here, moved the museum to larger quarters at 65th and Pulaski in the former Von Solberg Hospital building. A popular spot for tourists as well as locals, the museum also holds classes on many traditions of the Lithuanian culture.

In 1989, Mayor Eugene Sawyer led ground-breaking ceremonies for the 51st and South Pulaski station on the Southwest Transit Line. When completed in 1992, the long-anticipated Orange Line provided a direct link between Midway Airport and downtown Chicago. It was now possible for Chicago Lawners to hop on the Orange Line and be downtown in 20 minutes.

In May 1925, the first plane took off from a landing field at 63rd and Cicero, and the Chicago Municipal Airport was born. By 1941, the airport boasted nine runways. By 1959, it was the busiest airport in the world and had changed its name to Midway in recognition of the famous naval battle of World War II. In 1999, Midway announced a major multi-million-dollar expansion project to take the airport into the 21st century.

In 1941, the National Biscuit Company announced plans to build a huge bakery on the Southwest Side of Chicago. Once implemented, the plant housed the largest bakery in one location in the world. Located on the southern border of Chicago Lawn, NABISCO purchased and demolished the old Rheem Manufacturing building (in the forefront of the picture) in the late 1990s. With the construction of an additional facility here, NABISCO will double its size.

The Southwest Organizing Project evolved from the Catholic Cluster Project. Formed with the intention of unifying community institutions for common concerns, SWOP now boasts 26 member institutions of all faiths. Assemblies such as the one above bring elected officials and residents together to form solutions. Speaking at this May 2001 meeting were Speaker of the House Michael Madigan, Commissioner William Darr (at the podium), Rep. Daniel Burke, and Sen. Barrack Obama.

Notably the most highly publicized victory to date for SWOP has been that of predatory lending. Spurred by the number of seniors in the community falling prey to unscrupulous lending practices resulting in the loss of their homes, SWOP launched a campaign that included House Adoptions such as the one above, Loan Shark Attacks, Postcard Campaigns, trips to the legislature, and a visit from Gov. George Ryan.

The office of Neighborhood Housing Services came to Chicago Lawn at the invitation of GSDC, SWOP, and the Southwest Home Equity Assurance Program, bringing with them a vast array of services to homeowners and prospective buyers. While SWOP fought to end practices that brought homes into foreclosure, NHS stepped in, making their most invaluable contribution to date—the purchase and rehab of those foreclosed properties. Pictured here are the NHS board and staff in 2001.

Built in 1990, Churchview Manor sits on 63rd Street between Talman and Washtenaw. This project of Greater Southwest Development Corp. was designed to allow seniors who raised their families in the neighborhood the opportunity to stay in the community and still have comfortable maintenance-free housing. Before its doors opened, there was a substantial waiting list. Its sister development, Lawn Terrace at 63rd and Kedzie, even has its own indoor putting green.

The six Catholic institutions of Marquette Manor joined together in 1998, to form the Marquette Park Catholic Campus Council. Bishop John Gorman is pictured here at the installation of council delegates from St. Adrian Church, Holy Cross Hospital, Maria High School, Nativity BVM Church, Sisters of St. Casimir Motherhouse, and St. Rita of Cascia Parish.

The Gutierrez family walks down the street to Churchview Park quite often. Greater Southwest Development Corporation in conjunction with Chicago's Greenspace Program obtained the park, sitting on the corner of 63rd and Washtenaw, for the neighborhood. GSDC takes care of the maintenance, keeping it as a peaceful retreat on this busy street.

No longer a forum for racial tension, Marquette Park has gone back to its original purpose—a playground for the Southwest Side. The sign "Welcome to Marquette Park" is an invitation for all people to relish its vast beauty and indulge in its numerous activities, such as the new golf driving range which opened in 2001.

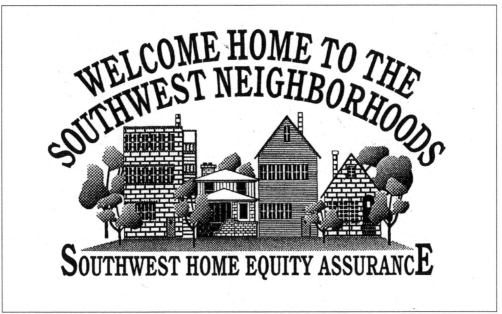

The Southwest Home Equity Assurance Program adopted this logo, making it into a decal for its members. Adorning the doors of Chicago Lawn and Marquette Manor residents, the decal speaks volumes as an outward sign to all who enter, encapsulating John Eberhart's original thought over 100 years ago, "This is where I want to live."

Acknowledgments

Sincere thanks and appreciation to my daughter Tracy for her immense help in preparing this book, and for the countless hours spent researching "just one more thing." Special thanks to the Chicago Lawn Historical Society, the *Southwest News-Herald*, and the Sisters of St. Casimir for opening up their archives and lending me their valuable photographs.

And thanks to the following people for their help with this book:

Helen Angonne
Joe Bagdzius
Lois Barr
Danute Bindakus
Joseph Boyle
Honorable Anne M Burke
James Capraro
Sr. Agnes Chapp SSC
Arthur Cholly
Dolores Czerwinski
Sr. Christella Danish
Kenneth Danz
Thomas Danz
Rita Dargis
Briget Ferriter
Christine Gencius

Sr. Jean Girzaitis SSC
Betty Gutierrez
Salvatore Gutierrez
Eulalie Hudson
John Jazecki
Helen Juozapavicius
Janice Kay
Jack Klaus
Sr. Alberta Kubilus SSC
Robert Kubkowski
Rev. William Lego OSA
Laverne Losos
Judy Malloy
Rev. Thomas McCarthy
　　OSA
Harry Meyer

Irma Morales
Dominic Pacyga
Sr. Therese Papsis SSC
James Parker
Leo Pocius
Lorelei Roth
Edward Rukis
Vida Sakevicius
John Stefanis
Peggy Stroger
Ryan Sullivan
James Volkman
James Vondrak
Sr. Immacula Wendt SSC
Sr. Margaret Zalot SSC

Finally, thanks to the stars of the pictures that have helped to tell the story of Chicago Lawn and Marquette Manor and made the communities what they are today.

CPSIA information can be obtained
at www.ICGtesting.com
Printed in the USA
LVOW03*0338310816
502548LV00012B/36/P